DECEPTION

Real or Fake News?

Dona Herweck Rice

J 070.43 Ric Main

Publishing Credits

Rachelle Cracchiolo, M.S.Ed., *Publisher*
Conni Medina, M.A.Ed., *Managing Editor*
Nika Fabienke, Ed.D., *Series Developer*
June Kikuchi, *Content Director*
Susan Daddis, M.A.Ed., *Editor*
Regina Frank, *Graphic Designer*

The TIME logo is a registered trademark of TIME Inc. Used under license.

Image Credits: p.8, p.22 illustrations by Jess Johnson; p.21 BSIP/
Fernando Da Cunha; p.27 Brian Cahn/Zuma Wire/Alamy Live News; all
other images from iStock and/or Shutterstock.

All companies and products mentioned in this book are registered
trademarks of their respective owners or developers and are used in
this book strictly for editorial purposes; no commercial claim to their
use is made by the author or the publisher.

Library of Congress Cataloging-in-Publication Data

Names: Rice, Dona author.
Title: Deception : real or fake news? / Dona Herweck Rice.
Description: Huntington Beach, CA : Teacher Created Materials, 2018. |
  Includes index.
Identifiers: LCCN 2017056305 (print) | LCCN 2018013015 (ebook) | ISBN
  9781425854706 (e-book) | ISBN 9781425849948 (pbk.)
Subjects: LCSH: Fake news--Juvenile literature. | Journalism--History--21st
  century--Juvenile literature. | Online journalism--Juvenile literature.
Classification: LCC PN4784.F27 (ebook) | LCC PN4784.F27 R53 2018 (print) |
  DDC 070.4/3--dc23
LC record available at https://lccn.loc.gov/2017056305

Teacher Created Materials
5301 Oceanus Drive
Huntington Beach, CA 92649-1030
www.tcmpub.com
ISBN 978-1-4258-4994-8
© 2019 Teacher Created Materials, Inc.
Printed in China
Nordica.052018.CA21800435

Table of Contents

Power of Deception

What if they find out?

How do I win?

What if they don't like me?

Most people say that honesty is the best policy; nonetheless, the art of deception is alive and well in the world. The proof is everywhere. In schoolyards, children deceive teachers to avoid getting into trouble. On billboards, print advertisements, and commercials, companies may deceive **consumers** to sell more products. In courtrooms, lawyers may deceive juries to help their clients be cleared of charges. In government offices around the world, politicians may use deception to **generate** more votes and support.

Honesty may be a good policy—but deception can rule the day.

Honesty Is the Best Policy

"Honesty is the best policy" is an old proverb. But no one knows exactly how old. The first known use of the phrase is in the writings of Sir Edwin Sandys, an English businessman and politician, in 1599. He included it in a book he wrote about religion in the Western world.

tted
ying
pace
cities
r the
lvers.

range
.stors.

vagen
with
tt, an
rator.

pple's
ailing
.xing.

500m
velop
g cars.

ow enough.

Power of Words

Merriam-Webster.com lists nearly 70 synonyms for *deception*. In contrast, there are fewer than 25 for *truth*.

For most of these countries oil is the main source of

Deception can be a tricky business, though. One lie may require more lies to protect it, and soon the deceiver is swimming in a sea of lies. And, of course, once someone begins to deceive others, it may become easier for that person to continue the practice.

Ironically, deception itself can be a deceiver, leading a person to believe that outcomes in life can be controlled. *If I lie*, the deceiver might think, *then I can make everything work out in my favor.*

It also takes tremendous effort to keep a lie going. Holes in stories tend to spring leaks, just like holes in a dam. The truth, as they say, is out there—and it has a way of coming forward.

So where is the real power? Is it in the truth—or does deception trump **reality**?

Truth Will Out

"Truth will out" is another common proverb about truth and deception. It means that the truth will become known eventually. William Shakespeare wrote the phrase in his 1596 play, *The Merchant of Venice*: "...truth will come to light; murder cannot be hid long; a man's son may, but at the length truth will out."

THINK LINK

Consider these questions to get to the truth about deception.

> In your experience, is it easier to maintain deception or truth? Why do you think that is so?

> What is the appeal of deception?

> Can deception ever be a worthwhile—or even moral—practice?

A World of Deception

Look around. Can you spot the deceptions? Advertisers reshape the truth, photographers alter pictures, and politicians make **dubious** claims. The lines between real and fake are easily blurred through technology, language, and more. "Lasts longer!" "Better than the rest!" "Nearly sold out!" "You must act now!" These and other attempts to shape reality can be found everywhere.

The average person may change his or her appearance with high heels, makeup, body-shaping undergarments, stylized facial hair, and more. Are these things deceptive—or do they simply enhance reality?

Notable & Quotable

"Seldom can it happen that something is not a little disguised, or a little mistaken."

—Jane Austen, author

Photoshop® software was invented in 1987. It was first sold to the public in the 1990s to make photographic images clearer. Now, the program is a standard tool for altering photographs. Anyone with the program and a computer can easily change images in a way that looks real.

Look closely at these two images. The first is an unaltered photo, and the second has been edited with Photoshop.

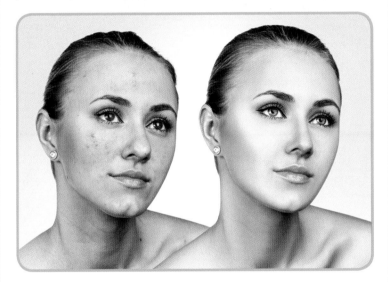

> Are you drawn to one image over the other? Explain why.

> Is editing an image **legitimate** for personal use? What about for use in a newspaper or news magazine? Why, or why not?

> Should it be legally required for a disclaimer to be printed with altered images so that it is clear that the image has been altered? Explain.

The purpose of advertising is to sell products or services; therefore, advertising claims can be misleading. For example, an ad may claim that four out of five dentists say that Toothpaste X is the best toothpaste. What that claim does not say is that the dentists surveyed are already Toothpaste X users. Perhaps they are all employees of the Toothpaste X company. Or maybe the whole **statistic** is just made up. After all, the truth can be hard to **verify**.

Sometimes, advertisers buy ad space that looks like news. It may say "paid advertisement" in small print, but the purpose is to fool consumers. Such ads are especially common on **social media**.

Hurry! Offer Ends Soon

Advertisers often use scare tactics to make a sale. They tell consumers that there is a special offer ending soon or that there is a very limited supply of a product. Consumers feel a sense of **urgency** to make purchases right away. But the truth may be that there is plenty available—or that the price was doubled before the small discount was applied.

WHITER TEETH
FRESHER BREATH
STRONGER GUMS

Recommended by
4 out of 5 dentists

Who Decides?

Advertising controls much of the **media**. Most companies pay for their ads to be on television or in magazines. Advertisers usually buy time or space in shows or magazines that fit what the companies think their customers will like.

Tooth

White

Fake News

Credible news sources should be truthful. However, anyone can create a news story on the Internet. Thanks to social media, those stories can easily reach millions of people. They may be "liked" or "shared" by those in positions of power or influence, which lends them credibility.

Real news can also be manipulated. It can be one-sided. Information may be left out. The news may also be presented as an **editorial** rather than informational.

Why would anyone create fake news? There are two main reasons. Some stories are meant to be **satire** and make people laugh or think. Not everyone understands them that way. Others are deceptions that are meant to influence votes or purchases.

Notable & Quotable

"Terrorism and deception are weapons not of the strong but of the weak."

—Mahatma Gandhi, sociopolitical leader

Cut! Print!

If you see footage of something, it must be true. Right? Not always. Video and film can be as easily manipulated as photographs. Pieces can be clipped out, sound can be altered, or sound or images can be added to change the content. Modern technology allows all of these edits and manipulations to seem completely authentic.

Wild World
NEWS WOW

ABRAHAM LINCOLN ADOPTS ALIEN BABY

President's Out of This World Family Photos Revealed!

Notable & Quotable

"Never assume the obvious
is true."

—*William Safire, journalist*

Information Literacy: Why It Matters

While examples of deception may be found everywhere, no one has to be a victim of it. People can learn to assess what they see, hear, and read and make judgments about information. This is not always easy. It can take some work and thought to figure out what is true. Sometimes, people who deceive others are banking on the idea that people do not want to do that much work. A careless population can make their job easy. But a **literate** population—one that reads and thinks for itself—can be bad news for deceivers. This is why people need to learn information literacy.

What exactly is *information literacy*? It is a set of skills. These skills give a person the ability to find, assess, understand, and use information that is shared in print, film, or other media.

Literacy Around the Globe

To find out how literate a country is, statisticians look at people 15 years of age or older who can read and write. In a 2015 study, the global literacy rate was about 86 percent. For men, it was 90 percent. The percentage for women was almost 83 percent.

There is more information available now than at any other time in history. But not all of it is valid. Some of it is made up, and some is mistaken. Many people believe that those who share information have a duty to make sure it is accurate. Others would say that consumers of information have obligations, too.

Responsibility of Journalists

The act of gathering and sharing news is called *journalism*. It is meant to give people information they need. Journalists are supposed to verify what they share. They should be accurate. They should also present all sides of an issue. Journalists are not meant to give opinions unless writing editorials. Even then, the writing should be supported with facts.

In Just One Second

Internet Live Stats is a website that keeps track of social media and the Internet. This site shows Internet activity captured every second. For example, in just one second the following activities took place:

- 7,768 tweets
- 804 Instagram® photos
- 2,777 Skype calls
- 70,907 YouTube™ viewings
- 62,698 Google searches

First Rule of Journalism

In the book *The Elements of Journalism*, the authors state that journalism's first obligation is to truth. They further write that information must be verified. That usually means that journalists need two sources to back up their findings. They must stay independent from those they write about. Last, they must monitor people in positions of power.

For most of these countri... ...il is the...

tted
ying
pace
cities
er the
ivers.

range
stors.

vagen
s with
tt, an
rator.

pple's
ailing
ixing.

500m
velop
g cars.

17

In order to make judgments about the news, people need to actively **engage** with it. They can then use reason to decide whether the news can be trusted.

Consumers may have one more responsibility. Today, anything can be liked or shared with the simple press of a button. What is shared can reach far and wide. Even if it is wrong, there is really no taking it back. Perhaps then the responsibility falls on everyone to share only what is valid. The widespread sharing of false information can have negative results for people and societies. If those who share news can separate fact from fiction, they may then help make society healthier.

Fairness Doctrine

In 1949, the Fairness Doctrine went into effect for TV and radio news. It stated that broadcast journalists were required to present all sides of an issue. Reporting had to be balanced and **nonpartisan**. The rule was overturned in 1987. That meant news could report just one side of an issue.

What Do You Think?

Katharine Graham, onetime owner of the *Washington Post* newspaper, said, "We live in a dirty and dangerous world. There are some things the general public does not need to know and shouldn't. I believe democracy flourishes when the government can take legitimate steps to keep its secrets and when the press can decide whether to print what it knows."

Please Like Me

People have a **fundamental** need to belong. They may dress or act like their peers, or they may join teams to fit in. In this way, they feel as though they are part of something bigger than themselves.

One way that people may seek to be accepted is through social media. They post photos and other updates that they hope will be "liked" and "shared." There is a sense of community that comes from this type of acceptance. Chemicals in the brain are also released when posts are liked. Dopamine is associated with feelings of pleasure. It is released when people eat good food or have a good laugh. It is also released when other people like what they share.

Because the need to be liked can be so strong, people may also be motivated to deceive in their sharing. They may want to look or sound better than they think they naturally do. The motivation to be liked may override the desire to be truthful.

Dopamine is sent from the brain to other nerve cells. It controls different functions. This diagram shows dopamine pathways in the brain.

Don't Get Fooled Again

How can a person avoid falling for deception? How can someone see through lies and **misinformation** to get to the truth?

It is not always easy. But there are useful things to remember that can help a person be a thoughtful receiver and sharer of news. First, just because something is said or written does not make it true. And just because someone in authority believes it, that also does not make it true. Even if many people respect that person, belief is never proof of fact. Proof is only found in credible evidence. It is never because someone says so.

Fool Me Once

There's an old saying that goes "Fool me once, shame on you. Fool me twice, shame on me." The idea is that people should learn from experience. This is true for news sources. If a source reports false or misleading information, consumers should be **skeptical** of that source in the future.

Facts vs. Opinions

To be a fact, something must be proven true. Even if everyone in the world believes something is true, it is not a fact until it has been proven.

Fact Checking

News organizations and publishers employ fact checkers to verify information. Even this book has been fact checked!

A U.S. representative made the news when he said, "Better to get your news directly from the president. In fact, it might be the only way to get the unvarnished truth." But is it really? One source, no matter who it is, cannot verify anything without evidence to support it. Power does not automatically equal truth.

Consumers can find out for themselves whether information is backed by credible sources. They can verify that the information has been fact checked. They can also check to be sure that primary sources match the information shared. Is it being reported accurately? Has the information been changed? Is key information left out? Consumers can find out all these things and more if they check sources themselves.

Primary Sources

Primary sources are often used to verify information. These sources are firsthand accounts of events. These can include news reports, letters, or journals. They also can be photographs and films, recordings, documents, or other artifacts that were created at the time in question. Primary sources are made or written by credible people who were present for the event.

Types of Information

Information can be presented in two main ways—news and opinion. Consumers can watch for certain **markers** to figure out which type of information it is. As long as they pay attention, it can be easy to tell.

News is meant to provide information based on facts. It does not have a **bias** in favor of any opinion. Opinions, on the other hand, are meant to persuade. They can also be based on facts, but mainly only the facts that support the opinion. Opinions may leave out or minimize facts that do not support the case. Also, look out for opinions that are made to look like news.

Totally Real News
1 min • 🌐

FOLLOW

YOU'LL NEVER BELIEVE THESE CELEBS' SECRET PASTS!

Clickbait

Often—and especially in social media—"news" headlines are written as clickbait. This is a modern term that describes very **enticing** headlines. The sole purpose is to get people to click on the link. These headlines usually lead to advertisements.

213,122 likes

ted
ving
pace
cities
r the
vers.

range
stors.

vagen
s with
tt, an
rator.

pple's
ailing
ixing.

500m
velop
cars.

ow enough.

Entertainment News

Entertainment is meant to interest and engage an audience. It may or may not use facts. Today, there are many shows and websites that are made to look and sound like news, but their purpose is to entertain. Real news may be shared, but it's usually for a laugh or to **rile** people up. Different sides of an issue are rarely included.

For most of these countries il is the in source of

News

If it looks like news, it is news—right? Not necessarily. Biased reporting, advertisements, false reports, and more can all be made to look like news. To know with certainty that something is news—and therefore accurate and worthwhile—the consumer should ask a few questions.

Who wrote the information? Legitimate news is written by a reporter whose name is shown in a **byline**. Online, that name usually links to the reporter's **credentials**. If there is no name, chances are good it is not real news.

When was it published? Legitimate news is listed with a date. Consequently, consumers can tell if the news is up-to-date.

Notable & Quotable

"The pressure to compete, the fear somebody else will make the first splash, creates a frenzied environment in which a blizzard of information is presented and serious questions may not be raised."

—*Carl Bernstein, investigative journalist*

THE DAILY NEWS

Supreme Court nominations expected
By: Tom Joyce
Published: May 28, 2018

The end of cheap oil
By: Nathan Nguyen
Published: May 28, 2018

Stock market hits new heights
By: Sarah Smith
Published: May 28, 2018

Proofreading Matters

Legitimate news is proofread. Not only is the information fact checked, but also the writing is checked for spelling and grammatical errors. The layout of the news is also professionally done. Mistakes and an amateur layout are clues that the information may be false news.

For most of these countries oil is the main source of

Is it from a credible news organization? Many news sources are well-known as legitimate. If unknown, the source should be researched. An online check can take little time and effort.

Are the story's sources named? **Reputable** (REH-pyuh-tuh-buhl) news will often include expert sources. These sources are named and information is given about what makes them experts. If facts are given without any source, consumers should be skeptical.

Is the headline neutral? Legitimate news usually gives no-nonsense headlines without biases. They are not **sensational** and do not make far-fetched claims. The headline simply states the topic and relevance of the information.

Wild World News
@wildworldnews

FOLLOW

Exclusive......Bigfoot barista spotted!!!!!

Trending now

30 536   1,369,945

Reply to @wildworldnews

Hoaxes

Some "news" sources are created solely to spread hoaxes. A hoax is a made-up story that is presented as true, in the hope of enticing and tricking people. Online, some of these stories get shared thousands—even millions—of times. What is a good way to check if something is a hoax? See if known, reputable news sources are reporting it. They usually do not report hoaxes.

REALITY CHECK

Real News
- byline
- dateline
- credible sources
- experts quoted
- neutral headline

Fake News
- no byline
- no date
- unreliable sources
- no sources or dubious sources
- biased headlines

Looks Can Be Deceiving

If a photograph that goes with an article doesn't seem quite real, it probably isn't. Techniques such as airbrushing are used to get rid of imperfections. Fake news often uses enhanced pictures to get the reader's attention.

The News Literacy Project

There is a wealth of information coming from all different directions and sources. It can be a challenge to navigate that information in a thoughtful way. The News Literacy Project (NLP) was created to help. The NLP "works with educators and journalists to teach middle school and high school students how to sort fact from fiction in the digital age." It is a nonprofit organization.

Checkology.org

The NLP offers an online program at https://checkology.org for middle and high school students. It takes between 15 and 20 hours to complete. Students can learn and apply the skills they need to determine what information is valid.

how to know what to believe

The following are some news organizations that partner with The NLP to support information literacy:

- ABC News
- Associated Press
- Bloomberg
- Buzzfeed
- CBS News
- *Chicago Sun-Times*
- *Chicago Tribune*
- CNN

- *Los Angeles Times*
- NBC News
- NPR
- *The New York Times*
- *USA Today*
- *The Wall Street Journal*
- *The Washington Post*

Why would a news organization want to be a part of The NLP? Why would it not?

Opinion

News may include opinions—but it should be clearly labeled as an *editorial* or *opinion piece*. However, plenty of information is shared under the **guise** of news that is actually an opinion.

How can you tell the difference? Here are some indicators to look for when deciding whether something is news or an opinion:

- Does it give you a strong emotional reaction?

- Is there a bias—an active support of one side of an issue?

- Can you tell what the reporter thinks about the topic?

If the answer to any of these is yes, it is not news. It is an opinion in disguise.

Notable & Quotable

"Journalism, as I was taught it, is a process of getting as close to some valid version of the truth as is humanly possible."

—*Dan Rather, journalist*

Editorial cartoons are also forms of opinion.

Validation

It is human nature to look for information that supports your biases. But journalism does not just back up people's biases. It challenges them. It provides a world of information and different viewpoints.

Persuasion and Advertising

Advertising is a type of opinion, and it is also intended to persuade. It is used to sell products or services. Facts may be included in advertisements, but if they are, they are only facts in favor of what is being sold.

Like all opinions, advertising wants the consumer to do something. How can you tell if something looks like news but is really an advertisement? Here are some key signs:

- There is no byline (no author or date).

- The source is a commercial business.

- There are no real facts or evidence.

- No one else is covering the same information.

- It may include words like "paid advertisement" or "sponsored."

It's in the Headline

Advertisements disguised as news will usually have headlines that are way too good to be true:

"Scientists Find the Secret of Youth!"

"You Just Might Be Able to Live Forever!"

"Man Wins Lottery 8 Times—and You Can, Too!"

Any of these outrageous headlines are sure signs that the content is an advertisement.

Caveat Emptor

Caveat emptor is a Latin expression. It means, "Let the buyer beware."

10 Ways Cleaning Technology Has Gotten Smarter

Sponsored ·

Like   Comment   Share

Write a comment...

Liar, Liar, Pants on Fire!

According to 30-year FBI agent, Mark Bouton, in his book *How to Spot Lies Like the FBI*, it is easy to spot a liar. Here's how:

◆ First, engage in some small talk with the person and watch how he or she acts. You will use that as a basis for comparing lying behavior to his or her normal behavior.

◆ Next, watch for the signs listed on these pages when you ask questions about suspected lies. If the person does not normally exhibit these behaviors, chances are good that he or she is lying.

Heavy sweating: Liars may perspire a lot.

Blushing: Women especially may blush after lying.

Rapid blinking: This is caused by stress.

Face touching: A chemical reaction when lying causes the face to itch, and liars will often touch or scratch their faces.

Looking directly to one side: Right-handed people look directly to their left when trying to remember something they heard. They look directly to their right when lying. The opposite is true for left-handed people.

Shifting eyes: This is a sign the person feels trapped and, even unconsciously, is looking for an escape.

Looking up to one side: Right-handed people look up to the left when finding a visual memory. They look up to the right when using their imagination. Left-handed people do the opposite.

Eyes that do not smile: Liars smile only with their mouths. The skin around their eyes does not wrinkle.

Pursed lips: Liars get a dry mouth and may purse their lips.

Blinks of a second or longer: This is a defense mechanism—almost like a child hiding when playing peek-a-boo.

The Bottom Line

There are many reasons for deception, both in print and in person. The bottom line is that one person is trying to make another believe something untrue or only partially true. People may play on emotions, invent information, misrepresent reality, and more in order to "prove" something and be accepted.

In the end, isn't that what it is all about—acceptance? Getting other people on your side, on your team? There is power in numbers—purchasing power, voting power, winning power.

If lies can get a person what he or she wants, is there any point in telling the truth? Or is it a case of "truth will out"? Like most things in life, each person must decide for himself or herself. Truth or deception? It's your call.

World of Lies

Experts tell us that we may be lied to up to two hundred times each day! They also claim that we personally lie—at least to some degree—in about one out of every five interactions we have.

Notable & Quotable

"The function of the press is very high. It is almost holy. It ought to serve as a forum for the people, through which the people may freely know what is going on. To misstate or suppress the news is a breach of trust."

—*Justice Louis D. Brandeis*

Glossary

bias—favoritism expressed toward one side of an issue

byline—news reporter's credit for authoring a piece

consumers—people who purchase or use products

credentials—education or experience that makes someone an expert

credible—trustworthy

dubious—causing doubt

editorial—an essay that gives a reporter's or an editor's opinion

engage—pay attention to and participate

enticing—attractive or tempting

fundamental—related to the most basic part of something

generate—create

guise—outward appearance

ironically—in a way that has the opposite meaning of what is expected

legitimate—conforming to accepted rules and standards

literate—able to read, write, and understand print

markers—signs

media—television, radio, the Internet, and print through which information is communicated

misinformation—false information

nonpartisan—not supporting one political party over another

reality—what is real and true

reputable—trustworthy

rile—anger

satire—humor that demonstrates weakness or foolishness in its subject

sensational—shocking or causing big excitement

skeptical—having doubt

social media—types of electronic communications through which people create groups to share information, photographs, ideas, and more

statistic—number that stands for information; data

urgency—the state of needing immediate action or attention

verify—prove true

Index

Check It Out!

Books

Ariely, Dan. 2013. *The Honest Truth About Dishonesty: How We Lie to Everyone—Especially Ourselves.* New York: Harper Perennial.

Lupica, Mike. 2016. *Fast Break.* New York: Puffin Books.

Paulsen, Gary. 2012. *Liar, Liar: The Theory, Practice and Destructive Properties of Deception.* New York: Yearling.

Videos

Rosenbaum, Jonathon A. 2014. *Pants on Fire.* Two 4 the Money Media.

Tempest, Marco. 2011. *The Magic of Truth and Lies (and iPods).* TED Talk.

Websites

The News Literacy Project.
www.thenewsliteracyproject.org.

Science News for Students.
www.sciencenewsforstudents.org.

Snopes. www.snopes.com.

TIME For Kids. www.timeforkids.com.

Try It!

You are the reporter! You are going to write an unbiased, informational news article on a controversial topic. It may be a challenge to keep your opinion out of the writing—but that is exactly what a good journalist does!

Here is what you do:

- ▶ Select a topic that intrigues you and about which you have a strong opinion.

- ▶ Research to find all the information you can on the topic. Be sure to check your sources for credibility.

- ▶ Write your article. Use only facts. Cite your sources.

- ▶ Ask a friend or a family member to read the article. Can they tell where you stand on the issue? If so, your bias is showing. Edit to see if you can remove it. If your bias does not show, you have succeeded in writing an unbiased news report!

SCHOOL NEWS

New Teachers, New Methods, New Tools...

Views on brand new trends in education

About the Author

Dona Herweck Rice has written hundreds of books for kids on all sorts of topics and under a dozen different pseudonyms. Her favorites are Howard Rice (her dog's name) and Elizabeth Austen, Nellie Wilder, and Anne Montgomery (named in tribute to her favorite authors and their classic book characters—can you figure them out?).

Rice delights in imagination—but has a particular aversion to deception that intends to coerce and manipulate people. For her, honesty is always a very good policy.

And that's the truth.